NONE
DARE
CALL
IT
TREASON!

BOOK 13

Big Business & Astounding Acts Of Treason!

Robert W. Pelton
$4.95

"Treason doth never prosper,

"What's the reason?

"Why if it prosper,

"None dare call it treason."

John Harrington

Printed in America
On Recycled Paper
In
Charleston, South Carolina

Published in America
By
The Freedom & Liberty
Foundation Press
Knoxville, Tennessee

Dedicated
To

The greatest, most generous, most benevolent and most powerful nation on the face of the earth – and the only country in the history of the world to have been founded on Biblical principles.

A nation can survive its fools, and even the ambitious. But it cannot survive treason from within.

An enemy at the gates is less formidable, for he is known and he carries his banners openly.

The traitor moves among those within the gates freely, his sly whispers rustling through the galleys, heard in the very hall of government itself.

For the traitor appears not traitor. He speaks in the accent familiar to his victims, and he wears their face and their garments, and he appeals to the baseness that lies deep in the hearts of all men.

He rots the soul of a nation - he works secretly and unknown in the night to undermine the pillars of a city - he infects the body politic so that it can no longer resist.

A murderer is less to be feared.

Cicero, 42 B.C.

Forward

Independence Hall Where the Declaration of Independence Was Signed.

Our glorious Declaration of Independence is a timeless divinely inspired masterpiece given to mankind through the anointed pen of Thomas Jefferson.

The grand and unmatched United States Constitution is indisputably the product of Providential guidance and wisdom and certainly not a document which evokes whimsical interpretations with the changing political climates.

All Americans have a moral obligation to stand up and be counted in these trying times!

Abraham Lincoln boldly declared: *"To sin by silence when they should protest, makes cowards of men."*

William Lloyd Garrison capsulized it best: *"As a free man who is determined to remain free -- I do not wish to think or speak, or write with moderation. "Tell a man whose house is on fire to give a moderate alarm; tell him to moderately rescue his wife from the hands of a ravisher; tell the mother to gradually extricate her babe from the fire into which it has fallen -- but urge me not to use moderation in a course like the present."*

Senator Barry Goldwater, 1964 Presidential candidate was castigated and verbally crucified by the media.

He simply stated this simple truism: *"Extremism in the pursuit of Liberty is no vice."*

This good and moral man of character soundly rocked the boat of the propagandists. He was as a result soundly defeated in the election.

The alarmed media wolves panicked the voters with their jeers and sneers and insane howls about this man's lack of *"moderation!"*

It can honestly be said that through the Providential genius of our Founding Fathers, the remaining remnants of the original American Constitutional Republic still provides more freedom, opportunity and abundance for mankind than is found in any other nation in the world.

This is true despite decade after decade of unabated treason and treachery promulgated by innumerable traitorous individuals found buried in the twiddle dee – twiddle dum administrations of both the Democrats and the Republicans.

 An informed and active, not a media brainwashed electorate, is the only antidote to further prostitution of, and the ultimate destruction of, what Benjamin Franklin called our Republic.

CONTENTS

Preface

"Treason against the United States shall consist only in levying war against them, or in adhering to their enemies, giving them aid and comfort."

U.S. Constitution. Article 111, Section 3

What is your treason I.Q.?

If you can answer the following questions, it's high.

If you miss one or more, you should read the *None Dare Call It Treason* series!

Who was behind allowing Red Chinese soldiers take airborne training at Fort Benning, Georgia?

Is this not treason?

Why was South Vietnam, South Africa, Rhodesia and numerous other American friends deliberately betrayed to the forces of evil?

Is this not treason?

Why was our friend Chiang Kai Shek not so gently coerced into a Communist dictatorship by highly placed subversives in the State Department?

Is this not treason?

Why was Cuba treasonously delivered into the clutches of Communist revolutionary Fidel Castro?

Is this not treason?

Why have untold millions of dollars consistently been used to prop up faltering Red dictatorships and to assist Communist terrorists in overthrowing non-Communist governments?

Is this not treason?

What American company sold nuclear reactors to Communist Occupied Romania?

Is this not treason?

Name the company that provided Communist Hungary with a factory designed to make 1.5 million light bulbs daily?

Is this not treason?

What well known oil company invested $1 billion for oil exploration in Communist Occupied Angola?

Is this not treason?

Can you name the American company who treasonously built and equipped a $10 million electronics plant near Warsaw for the Polish slave labor tyranny?

Is this not treason?

These are questions to which every American should rightfully have an honest answer.

Unfortunately most do not!

Tragedy was carefully orchestrated by traitors in our Government and the media with regard to Cuba, Vietnam, Laos, Cambodia, Rhodesia, China, El Salvador, Nicaragua and many other countries.   Anastasio   Somoza was the former President of free Nicaragua.

He offered this startling insight in his 1980 book, Nicaragua Betrayed: *"I have factual evidence that the betrayal of Nicaragua was not perpetrated out of ignorance, but rather by design."*

Somoza was soon after assassinated!

Is this not treason?

John Lehman, Secretary of the Navy, made this shocking statement on May 25 to the 1983 Annapolis graduating class: *"Within weeks many of you will be looking across just hundreds of feet of water at some of the most modern technology ever invented in America.*

"Unfortunately, it is on Soviet ships."

Is this not treason?

Earl E.T. Smith was the American   Ambassador   to

Cuba when it was similarly delivered to the Communists.

He makes this concise comment on July 14, 1986: *"Nicaragua is Cuba all over again."*

Can you name the company that paid the Communist dictatorship in Angola over $600 million annually in taxes and oil royalties.

This money bought new Soviet jets, tanks and helicopter gunships.

And it paid Castro for supplying 35,000 imported Cuban mercenaries who keep the Angolan people enslaved.

Is this not treason?

Stressed retired Brigadier General Andrew J. Gatsis on August 11, 1986: *"Though aware of the Communist goal of world domination, the average U.S. Citizen refuses to believe that the real threat comes*

from governmental officials and their non-governmental confederates who secretly espouse the same objectives as the openly avowed Communists."

Anthony Sutton stated in his 1986 book *The Best Enemy Money Can Buy: "We now have the formidable task of bringing these gentlemen to the bar of justice to publicly answer for their private and concealed actions."*

The *None Dare Call It Treason* series certainly won't win accolades from the United Nations or the State Department!

Nor will Harvard feel compelled to bestow an honorary degree upon the author!

Harvard Law School was the spawning ground for an incredible number of Red agents. Included were members of the first Soviet spy ring ever to be exposed in our government.

Reed Irvine aptly commented in July of 1986: *"Indeed, it has long been a joke among refugees from Eastern Europe that there are more Marxists at Harvard than there are in the Soviet Union, or Poland, or whatever Communist country the refugee called home."*

The Honorable Ezra Taft Benson said:

 *"The truth must be told even at the risk of destroying, in large measure, the influence of men who are widely respected and loved by the American people.*

"The stakes are high. Freedom and survival is the issue."

Treason is still a most serious federal offense.

The *None Dare Call It Treason* series examines the reasons for and the Americans behind the fall of freedom and the rise of tyranny throughout the world!

Has anything really changed?
You Decide!

Treason

Whoever, owing allegiance to the United States, levies war against them or adheres to their enemies, giving them aid and comfort within the United States or elsewhere, is guilty of treason and shall suffer death, or be imprisoned not less than five years and fined not less than $10,000; and shall be incapable of holding any office under the United states.

U.S. Code, Title 18, Section 2381

Whoever, owing allegiance to the United States and having knowledge of the commission of any treason against them, conceals and does not, as soon as may be, disclose and make known the same to the President or to some judge of the United States, or to the Governor or to some judge or justice of a particular state, is guilty of misprision of treason, and shall be fined not more than $1000 or imprisoned not more than 7 years or both.

U.S. Code, Title 18, Section 2382

Big
Business
&
Astounding Acts
of
Treason!

Treason: *"The act of helping its [one's country] enemies."*

The New Horizon Ladder Dictionary

An outwardly friendly, handshaking, smiling, but highly dangerous Russian fox visited the United States in December 1987.

He glibly spoke to a gathering of American business entrepreneurs.

One trusting rabbit in the audience stood and enthusiastically vocalized: *"You're a nice guy Mr. Fox!*

"We really like you!

"We're going to enjoy doing business with you!"

And the wily Red Fox hungrily licked his lips while his eyes glistened in anticipation.

This is the Mikhail Gorbachev who President Reagan said was *"completely different from previous Soviet leaders."*

It's the Mikhail Gorbachev who was still running a brutal Communist dictatorship holding upwards of 15 million slave laborers in some 2,000 ungodly concentration camps throughout the Soviet Union.

It's the same Mikhail Gorbachev who was still holding American POWs from the Korean War in some of these slave labor camps!

And it's the same Mikhail Gorbachev who, one month earlier in Moscow had stated: *"In October 1917, we parted with the Old World, rejecting it once and for all.*

"We are moving toward a new world, the world of Communism.

"We shall never turn off that road."

The dangers of doing business with Red dictatorships are obvious.

A frightening torrent of American technology continued to flow to Communist occupied nations.

These criminal regimes were shipped anything and everything they wanted.

Complete turnkey factories had gone to Russia.

Nuclear power plants to Communist Occupied Yugoslavia.

Automated steel mills to Red China.

Such activity is *clearly* in the realm of treason!

Nevertheless, an unbelievable array of greedy American businesses choose to illegally aid and abet the various Red slave states.

American companies sell Communist Occupied Russia and other satellite slave dictatorships machinery, complete factories and other equipment.

Maintenance contracts, service manuals and training materials are included.

Instructors are loaned to Communist tyrannies to teach their workers.

Red bloc technicians and scientists are even trained in the United States.

Dr. Miles Costick points out that as of 1976, the Soviets had been able to obtain from the West around 1,000 *"turn-key"* factories and plants.

Here are a few of the other culprits who have done (or are presently doing) business with Communist slave states: American Can; American Express; Atchison, Topeka & Santa Fe Railway; Atlantic Richfield; Avon Products; Bendix Corporation; Borg-Warner; Caterpillar Tractor; Chrysler Corporation; Firestone; The Hartford Insurance Group; International Harvester; IT&T; National Cash Register; Reynolds Metal; Sheraton International; Singer.

There are hundreds more!

PepsiCo's Donald Kendall wrangled a monopoly from Communist Occupied Russia.

Paul Austin got Coca Cola the same deal in Communist Occupied China.

Terrorist revolutionary Vladimir Ilich Ulyanov *(pseudonym: N. Lenin)* long ago correctly prophesied: *"The Capitalists of the world will close their eyes and thus will turn into deaf, mute, blind men.*

32

"Giving us the materials and technologies we lack, they will restore our military industry, indispensable for our future victorious attacks on our suppliers.

"They will labor for the preparation for their own suicide."

Marvelous Bolshevik achievements boasted about by American leftists in the 1930s were no more than a figment of their fertile imaginations.

Such glorified accomplishments were 100-percent nonexistent!

They were pure propaganda!

As are current tales about purported Soviet space triumphs and industrial growth!

Everything was and still is the product of despised capitalistic ingenuity, money and know how.

Every factory, *every* plant, *every* scientific advance resulted from American and Western European technology transfers to Communist Occupied Russia.

Few Americans realize that the USSR is still one of the world's most backward nations.

Larry Abraham was right on target when he stated in March of 1987: *"Soviet economic, technological, and scientific achievements are non-existent.*

"Were it not for the West, the Soviet Union would be so primitive as to be the laughing stock of the world."

Congressman John Ashbrook pointed on July 22, 1967: *"In order to enjoy the glories of the present Soviet system, we would have to*

abandon three-fifths of our steel capacity, two-thirds of our petroleum production, 95 percent of our electric motor output, destroy two out of every three of our hydroelectric plants, and get along on a tenth of our present volume of natural gas.

"We would have to rip up 14 of every 15 miles of paved highways and two of every three miles of our mainline railroad tracks.

"We would have to destroy 18 of every 20 cars.

"We would cut our living standard by three-fourths, destroy 40 million TV sets, nine

out of every 10 telephones, and seven of every 10 houses; and then we would have to put about 60 million of our people back on the farm."

Occidental Petroleum's notorious Armand Hammer has been a pal of various U.S. Presidents and patron of all Russian dictators from Lenin to present.

His father was a personal friend of the goateed ghoul and a founder of the American Communist Party.

This well-connected man went to the Soviet Union in 1921 with a large shipment of goods to help prop up the faltering Red dictatorship.

Hammer's reward was a monopoly on the manufacture of slave-made pens and pencils in Communist Occupied Russia.

Over a million dollars in blood money was netted the first year.

He went on to build huge chemical plants in the USSR and made many other treasonous deals with his Kremlin pals.

Hammer's American Allied Drug and Chemical Company had the concession for mining asbestos in the Urals. This was but another monstrous slave labor enterprise.

His company was one of the first U.S. firms to open an office in Moscow.

Averill Harriman was another multi-millionaire American businessman who goes way back with his many Soviet buddies.

In 1920, he founded W.A. Harriman & Company. His banking firm immediately granted loans to Bolshevik leader V.I. Lenin in order to keep the Communist terrorists in power.

In 1925 this man paid his Kremlin bosses $3.45 million for the Georgian manganese concessions.

He thereby obtained the exclusive right to mine and export manganese ore.

How many slave laborers were forced to dig the ore in Harriman's Russian mines?

How many slave labor deaths can be attributed to Ambassador Harriman's manganese mining venture?

Mack Truck sold $25 Million worth of heavy equipment for use in Soviet mining operations.

How many slave laborers were forced to use Mack equipment?

Ford Motor Company sold 20,000 tractors and replacement parts to the Soviet Union between 1922 and 1926.

More than 85 percent of all tractors and trucks in 1927 Communist Occupied Russia had been built by Ford in Detroit.

Then, in 1929, the USSR purchased $30 million worth of automobiles and repair parts from the Ford company.

The early 1930s saw U.S. firms stumbling all over themselves in an attempt to help shore up the floundering Soviet police state.

Included were such American stalwarts as RCA, Douglas Aircraft, Westinghouse and DuPont.

A plant was designed and constructed by United Engineering to manufacture the aluminum sheets used in Russian planes.

Kharkov was the site where GE built Communist Occupied Russia a huge turbine electric producing facility.

Its capacity was nearly three times that of General Electric's massive plant in Schenectady, New York.

A carbon copy of the Gary, Indiana, steel making complex was built in Magnitogorsk for Communist Occupied Russia.

Employees of the Arthur G. McKee Company in Cleveland, Ohio, supervised the slave labor used to build the Soviet version!

The Koppers Corporation contracted to supply the coke ovens.

During this same period, Standard Oil and other American firms supplied the Soviet Union with $37 million worth of equipment and machinery.

Moscow was the site of the American built MORNING steel making complex.

Then there was the infamous deal made for the Stalingrad Tractor Plant.

This factory was fully erected in the United States, disassembled and then shipped to Communist Occupied Russia.

American engineers actually supervised the slave laborers assigned to reconstruct the plant in Stalingrad!

Over 80 U.S. companies greedily supplied equipment for this project.

Tractor factories were built in Chelyabinsk by the John K Calder Company of Detroit.

Nitric acid plants were constructed for the Reds by Dupont.

In 1967, Communist Occupied Russia's despotic Aleksei N. Kosygin visited the United States.

He was asked: *"With all the talk about friendship, peace, and 'building bridges,' does the Soviet Union still have as its primary objective the overthrow of capitalism?"*

His brazen response was immediate: *"Of course!"*

The Nixon-Kissinger team gave Most Favored Nation trade status to Communist Occupied Russia in 1972.

The Soviet enemy was thereby guaranteed an endless deluge of food, machinery, industrial plants, complete factories and military goods.

Carl Gerstacker who was at the time Chairman of Dow suggested in *Ford Engineering* of May !967, that an expansion of trade with Communist nations is *"highly desirable."*

He also goes a step further and hints that Communist nations *should* be allowed to bid on government projects in the U.S.

American Cyanamid Executive Vice President Robert C. Swain agreed: *"It is possible we will see a Soviet owned and operated plant on U.S. soil.*

"It is also possible that the next generation of business leaders in the United States will be choosing sites in the Soviet Union for their plant operations."

Swain was right!

Control Data Corporation signed a 10-year agreement with the Soviet State Ministry of Science and Technology in 1973.

Included was an agreement to jointly develop a super computer!

General Electric admitted their contract for electric power technology would bring *"hundreds of millions of dollars worth of business."*

Also grabbing a lucrative piece of the action was the Bechtel Corporation of San Francisco.

This was the firm employing the men who were to eventually become Reagan's Secretary of State and Secretary of Defense.

In June 1973, Armand Hammer's Occidental Petroleum contracted with Communist Occupied Russia to run a 2,000 mile natural gas line across Siberia to Vladivostok.

El Paso Natural Gas Company joined Occidental in this treasonous $10 billion project!

Irrefutable evidence proved Communist Occupied Russia's Siberian natural gas pipeline was being constructed with slave labor.

At least 50 crude concentration camps were built by Finnish contractors.

These *"villages"* were to house the slave laborers brought in to work on the project.

Sparsely dressed men, women, and children were forced to work a 16-hour day, in below-zero weather.

Despite this, another Soviet natural gas line was contracted to run from western Siberian gas fields to the port of Murmansk.

"Project Northstar" was undertaken by three American firms -- Brown & Root, Tenneco, and Texas Eastern Transmission.

Charged William P. Hoar in May of !974: *"Western capitalists are helping to dig their own graves by making possible the largest East-West deal ever -- the Soviet gas pipeline that will make Europe dependent on the Kremlin for energy."*

43

The United States faced a serious energy shortage in 1973.

Instead of using scarce oil drilling equipment to help solve the energy dependence problem in America the Nixon Administration traitorously peddled the badly needed items to Communist Occupied Russia.

America's enemies were sold on credit around a billion dollars worth all financed by U.S. taxpayers.

Some of the firms involved:

International Harvester $42 million worth of crawler tractors for pipeline construction

Kendall Polychem thousands of tons of pipeline coating.

Dresser Industries and Halliburton-Welex $3.5 million worth of various exploration items.

Business Week of December 8, !973, reported: *"A severe shortage of drilling pipe and well casing"* resulted in tens of thousands of oil wells not being drilled in the U.S. even though there was an energy crisis.

Congressman John Ashbrook suggested with a tinge of sarcasm: *"Perhaps after we have finished developing the Soviet economy, we can then turn to our own needs."*

The World Trade Center or *"Traitor Inn"* was paid for with American money and built in Moscow by Bechtel.

Treason?

What else could it be labeled?

Shadowy security risk Armand Hammer arranged the sweetheart deal.

His Occidental Petroleum snared a lucrative $110 million contract for this monument to his KGB pals.

All of the guest rooms were outfitted by Holiday Inns of America.

A few of the firms listed on the Building Directory are Control Data Corporation, 2006; Chase Manhattan Bank NA, 1709; Bank of America, 1605; Occidental Petroleum, 1409; Ingersoll-Rand Company, 1101; and Allis-Chalmers Corp, 901.

U.S. News & World Report of December 18, 1978, described America's traitorous participation in building

45

Communist Occupied Russia's spectacular 36 square mile conglomerate known as the Kama River Truck Factory: *"The plant contains more than 1 billion dollars worth of Western-made machinery.*

"The list of the 40 U.S. companies that have had a hand in the project reads like a roll call of blue chip stocks.

"Without this U.S. participation, no one involved in the venture doubts that it would have remained on the drawing board for many years."

The Commerce Department's Office of Export Control refused to identify the U.S. firms involved in the militarily invaluable Kama River venture.

According to these bureaucrats, the names of participants had to be kept secret as a matter of *"national security"* per Section 7(c) of the *Export Administration Act.*

Legal counsel William N. Letson said that making the names public *"could lead to criticism and even economic pressure directed against specific private companies by persons who oppose the government's general policy on trade with Communist countries in non-strategic commodities. "*

In other words, patriotic American citizens might just boycott such firms!

And they just might view such outrageous activities as blatant acts of treason!

The prime contractor was Swindell-Dressler of Pittsburgh, a subsidiary of Pullman Incorporated.

Swindell-Dressler was among the first U.S. industrial firms to open a branch office in Moscow.

They received a fat $190 million to design the arc furnaces and the foundry equipment.

Here are a few of the other *"patriotic"* money-hungry American companies taking part in this questionable *"non-military"* project:

Combustion Engineering got a $30 million contract to supply molding machines.

Ingersoll Milling Machine Company supplied the automated equipment needed to hone diesel engine blocks.

Their take: $19 million.

Also heavily involved in this treasonous project were Westinghouse, IBM, Honeywell, and General Motors.

"The Soviets were allowed to acquire the most advanced American technology in computers, inertial guidance, semi-conductors, high-propulsion, and wide-bodied aircraft," charged Major General George Keegan retired Air Force Chief of Intelligence.

He revealed in September of 1977 that the Commerce Department had *destroyed official records* on trade with Communist Occupied Russia and the Red Bloc slave states.

Why else but to cover deliberate, massive acts of treason?

The destruction of such records clearly indicates that the traitors are more than a little concerned!

The leftists know they've committed treason!

What else could it be called to give them guidance systems to make their missiles more accurate?

To supply them with extremely sophisticated computers to run a missile defense system for protecting their cities?

To build them military truck and tank factories?

To sell them advanced jet fighters?

To train their pilots to fly them?

And ad infinitum!

"The Soviet computer industry has always been a shambles," said Wade Holland on July 16, 1976.

He was the editor of Rand Corporation's *Soviet Cybernetics Review.*

The first American computer sale to Communist Occupied Russia took place in 1959.

It was a Model-802 National sold by Elliott Automation, a British subsidiary of General Electric!

Sperry Rand Corporation was big on computer sales to Communist dictatorships.

On April 15, 1979, President Carter personally approved the sale of a highly sophisticated Sperry Rand computer to *Tass,* the KGB controlled Soviet news agency.

Honeywell had long been supplying computers to the Reds.

IBM sold Intourist a computerized reservation system revealed Time on July 16, 1973.

This was exactly what the government-run travel agency needed to assemble dossiers on foreign visitors.

Computers used by the dreaded KGB are also American made.

The Russians got them by saying they were needed by Aeroflot for ticket reservations.

Figures obtained from the Department of Commerce give a pretty good idea of how far American computer companies have gone down the treason road.

From 1975 to 1979, U.S. firms sold Communist Occupied Russia $300 million worth of computers and related materials.

In just one six-month period ending on April fool's Day 1978 almost $43 million worth of American computer hardware had been sold to the Soviet enemy.

"How sickeningly ironical it would be if American computers would keep track of political prisoners," said Carl Olson in April of 1989.

This man was chairman of Stockholders for World Freedom, *"Or that*

American pipe-laying equipment would be manned by Vietnamese forced-labor gangs working on the Siberian gas pipeline."

This is exactly what happened!

Allis-Chalmers contracted to build a $35 million plant in Communist Occupied Russia for pelletizing iron ore.

The factory is one of the largest of its kind in the world.

According to United Press International (UPI) on September 18, 1973: *"The equipment to be used in the new Soviet plant will include some of the most advanced in the technology of converting iron ore into pellets, which are used for steel making."*

The C.E. Lummus Company of Bloomfield, New Jersey, agreed to build Communist Occupied Russia a huge petrochemical plant in the Ukraine.

The cost: $105 million.

The Soviets erected the building using the usual slave labor crews.

The Lummus Company provided the engineering design, supervision and all the necessary equipment.

Monsanto also involved in the deal sold the Soviets their latest technical data on the production of acetic acid.

"The military potential of the industrial plants we are building for the Soviets should be obvious to anyone," offered Gary Allen in May of 1974. *"Trucks, aircraft, oil, steel, petrochemicals, aluminum, computers -- these are the sinews of a military-industrial complex.*

"These factories, the product of American genius and financed by American capital, could have been built in the United States.

"Instead, they are constructed at the U.S. taxpayer's expense in the Soviet Union a nation whose masters still keep millions in concentration camps and who have sworn to bury us."

In December 1979, Armco Incorporated received a marvelous Christmas gift from America's atheistic *"friends."*

They nailed down a contract to build a fully automated electrical steel mill in Communist Occupied Russia.

The cost: $353 million!

During Carter's peak years, over 60 American firms had lucrative but propitious science and technology transfer contracts with Communist Occupied Russia.

Incredibly, these included three key U.S. defense contractors: General Dynamics and Litton *(both build nuclear submarines),* and Union Carbide.

Leading computer firms involved were Hewlett-Packard, IBM, and Sperry Rand.

The wiley Russians actually had America's major aerospace firms -- Boeing, Lockheed, and McDonnell Douglas -- in a building war to supply them with wide-bodied planes.

Bechtel was another -- then run by Reagan's Defense Secretary Casper Weinberger (CFR) and Secretary of State Shultz (CFR).

The Reagan Administration ignored the widespread Soviet slave labor practices and authorized a $90 million sale of 200 pipe laying bulldozers for use on their Siberian pipeline.

Soviet exile Mikhail Makarenko explained in November of 1982 how slave labor was to be utilized on the 3,600 mile construction project: *"They will be the ones who will clear the forests, build the roads and the first living quarters for the more skilled specialists who will put the pipeline in place.*

"It's going to be human bodies that will thaw this unbelievable tundra through which the pipeline will be built.

"Today in the Soviet Union you have 2,000 camps and prison; 150 are for women and children under two.

"Hundreds of other camps are for children from 11 to 18 years of age, and many

of these prisoners will be working on the pipeline."

Senator Jesse Helms was against this sale. He charged on June 24, 1981, that the special bulldozers *"could be used to lay coaxial cable for hardened, underground communications networks for military command structures, ABM systems, etc."*

Howard Hughes was a vocal anti-Communist.

He might well roll over in his grave if he knew the Hughes Tool Company was selling offshore exploration equipment to Communist Occupied Russia.

This firm sold $40 million worth of high-tech submersible pumps.

On March 6, 1984, President Reagan approved the sale.

"We have already sent to the Soviet Union tremendously sophisticated machinery which," charged Senator Steven D. Symms in October of 1974, *"under their own system of*

suppressing individual ingenuity, would have taken years if not decades to develop.

"The flow of advanced technology from the United States to the Soviet Union has rapidly turned into a frightening torrent."

Despite the Soviet Union's horrifying human right record -- unspeakable brutality, wholesale rape, mass murder, assassination, terrorism, and slavery -- 40 Russian trade officials were cordially invited to the United States in May 1984.

These Communist malefactors were to meet with American members of the US-USSR Trade and Economic Council.

The USTEC was organized in 1973 with the unqualified backing of Kremlin despot Leonid Brezhnev.

It was conceived for one purpose only and that was to supply the Soviet enemy with the latest American technology.

USTEC has hundreds of important supporters in the U.S. corporate community.

Half of USTEC's board of directors is staffed by Russian government officials.

The Soviet officials were told that American corporations were willing to ship

Communist Occupied Russia such things as fertilizers, fuels, trucks, bulldozers, metals, and complete manufacturing plant packages.

On December 21, 1987 Senator Helms charged the USTEC with being *"an arm of the Soviet Government, under KGB control, whose purpose is to subvert the U.S. economy."*

In early December 1985 400 business leaders representing 150 major American corporations made a perfidious trek to Moscow.

Commerce Secretary Malcolm Baldridge arrogantly refused to reveal the names of the companies.

Nor would he tell what kinds of technology and strategic goods these firms were selling to the Communists.

No doubt the Commerce Secretary's greedy traveling companions welcomed his discretion.

But surely these corporate leaders knew they were committing treason!

Whether it's government sanctioned or not is beside the point.

Treason is treason!

But their desire to participate secretly is certainly understandable.

Infuriated at this bureaucratic secrecy, Senator Helms indignantly declared: *"The Soviets know, the Commerce Department knows, and the Banking Committee knows. But nobody else is supposed to know, least of all the American people whose liberty and security may be at stake in this matter."*

A 1983 Heritage Foundation study unequivocally showed the Kremlin gaining the military edge over the U.S.

This was caused by *"a virtual hemorrhage of technology in the past decade"* flowing steadily from America to Communist Occupied Russia.

The culprits included such companies as General Motors, Xerox, and Exxon -- all of whom do big business with the Reds!

The USSR had with the treacherous assistance of America's leaders come to a point where it could zap half the population in the United States more quickly than it took to declare war in 1941 after Pearl Harbor was bombed!

American fighting men in Vietnam were being maimed and murdered by North Vietnamese soldiers and Communist Vietcong terrorists.

The North Vietnamese war effort was almost entirely subsidized by the United States and other Western nations through aid to Communist Occupied Russia and its numerous slave state satellites.

Nothing critical was to be said of those firms who were indirectly supplying weapons and war materials to the Vietnamese enemy with whom America was waging a war.

At the same time subversive elements in the State Department made it appear that

American businessmen who aided and abetted the Reds were patriots rather than traitors!

State Department traitors tried to make the public believe that concerned citizens who protested the supplying of weapons and war materials to the enemy were guilty of un-American activities!

State Department document 8117, *Private Boycotts vs The National Interest* dated August of 1986 contained this ominous warning: *"All American citizens should know that any American businessman who chooses to engage in peaceful trade with the Soviet Union or Eastern European countries [satellite Communist dictatorships] is following the policy of his government.*

"Any organization, however patriotic in intention, that undertakes to boycott or blacklist any American business for engaging in peaceful trade with Eastern European countries or the Soviet Union, is acting against the interests of the United states."

Don't these traitors know that communist bestiality knows no limitations?

Are they ignorant of the fact that Communist ruthlessness has no conscience?

Do they not realize that Communist action precludes no morality?

"Patriotism means to stand by the country" chided Theodore Roosevelt. *"It does not mean to stand by the President or any other public official save exactly to the degree in which he himself stands by the country."*

Here's a perfect example of how a typical Communist blandly views murder, deceit, and immorality.

William C. Bullitt was the American Ambassador to the Soviet Union in 1934.

He was seated at dinner one evening between Marshal Budenny and General Kliment Voroshilov.

Referring to Budenny, Voroshilov turned to Bullitt and said: *"I think the most extraordinary thing we ever did together was to capture Kiev without fighting.*

"There were 11,000 Czarist officers with their wives and children in Kiev and they had more troops than we had.

"We told them that they would be released and allowed to go to their homes with their families and treated as well as possible by our army, and they believed us and surrendered."

"What did you do then?" asked Bullitt.

"Oh," responded Voroshilov, *"we shot all the men and boys and we put all the women and the girls into brothels for our army."*

"Do you think that was a very decent thing to do?" Bullitt queried in astonishment.

"My army needed women," said Voroshilov matter of factly, *"and I was concerned by my army's health and not with the health of those women; and it didn't make any difference anyhow, because they were all dead within three months."*

It was once illegal for American firms to sell advanced technology and strategic goods to enemy nations.

Specifically prohibited were sales to Communist Occupied Russia and other Red slave dictatorships.

Despite the horrors reported by Ambassador William C. Bullitt, this dramatically changed under the Kennedy Presidency.

The spigot for direct sales of high-tech/strategic goods and dangerous government giveaways began.

The criminal policy of aiding and abetting the enemy was accelerated during Johnson's reign.

It continued under Nixon, Ford, Carter, and Reagan.

There's virtually nothing American businesses cannot now sell to the totalitarian enemies of freedom.

For example, in May of 1974, General Electric was preparing to build Communist Occupied Yugoslavia a nuclear power plant!

The cost: $250 million!

The United States paid the bill!

A $75 million radial tire factory was constructed in Communist Occupied Romania by General Tire.

This company was later doing business with the Marxists-Leninist thugs in Communist Occupied Angola.

Other American firms making huge profits in Red Romania included IBM, GE, Pepsi-Cola, and Phillip Brothers.

Corning Glass in upstate New York provided Janos Kadar's Red dictatorship with a light bulb factory.

This automated plant can produce 1.5 million light bulbs daily. Many are exported and sold to unsuspecting American consumers.

The Corning people don't seem to be bothered by the fact that Communist Occupied Hungary openly deals in slave trade with their Soviet masters and with Communist China as well.

According to a 1956 German church publication called *Christ Und Wedlt*, troublesome able-bodied Hungarians were sold to Moscow like cattle. The price was approximately $100 a head and to Peking for $150 each!

The formal contracts call these slave laborers *"specialized workers assisting in social reconstruction."*

Facts on File of March 1974 revealed: *"The Dow Chemical Company, the first U.S. company to set up an office in East Berlin, signed a 10-year contract with East Germany."*

Malcolm W. Browne wrote of Czechoslovakia in the *New York Times* of January 25, 1977: *"In the Bohemian town of Obernica, American engineers and technicians of the Union Carbide Corporation have been supervising construction of a polyethylene plant."*

The number of treasonous computer sales to Soviet puppet dictatorships has been absolutely astounding!

During one six month period from October 1977 through March 1978 American companies sold the Reds almost $50 million worth.

And business has been booming ever since then.

Here's the breakdown:

Communist Occupied Bulgaria $1,188,421

Communist Occupied East Germany $2,195,770

Communist Occupied Hungary $7,718,453

Communist Occupied Latvia $249,720

Communist Occupied Poland $10,805,896

Communist Occupied Romania $6,158,730

"I'm profoundly opposed to the trade or transfer of scarce technology with military applications," said Ambassador Jeanne J.  Kirkpatrick in January of 1986. *"There are laws against the transfer of certain technology to the Communist Bloc, and I think they should be enforced."*

Many companies play the *Help-the-Soviet Satellite-Game.*

Communist Occupied Poland appears to be a favorite of American business entrepreneurs.

Westinghouse designed and equipped a $10 million electronics plant near Warsaw for the Polish slave-labor tyranny.

Angola was taken over by Moscow backed terrorists in 1975.

Chevron-Gulf immediately contracted with the barbaric Red dictatorship for exploration and production in the oil rich Cabinda Province.

Chevron-Gulf is responsible for about 90 percent of the oil pumped for the hostile Communist military regime.

Many other stalwart American companies greedily grabbed a piece of the action!

These include Cities Service, Texaco, Mobil, Exxon, Union, Marathon, Texas Petroleum and Conoco.

Westinghouse also scrambled to get in on the lucrative business opportunities soon after the Reds occupied Angola.

They contracted to repair, modernize, and replace radar installations at Angolan airfields.

Westinghouse people worked under relatively safe conditions.

Combat-hardened Cuban troops were brought in to guard the areas.

In 1981, Chevron-Gulf announced its intention to invest $1 billion for oil exploration in Communist Occupied Angola over a five year period.

Here we have a unique situation.

Westinghouse was still treasonously aiding and abetting the Red enemy in September 1981.

With Free World financing and Westinghouse technology, Communist Occupied Yugoslavia's first nuclear power plant went operational.

General Electric sold Romania two nuclear reactors!

The Soviets supplied Red Angola with $2 billion worth of military equipment, guns, and ammunition in 1984-85 alone.

Some of the biggest corporations in the U.S. paid for much of this with oil revenues!

In 1979, RCA got a $68 million equipment and technology contract. They began producing color television  tubes in their Polish factory.

RCA operated a similar plant in the Soviet Union.

Control Data Corporation went into a business partnership with the Romanian Reds. They treasonously built a computer factory in Bucharest at a cost of $2.2 million.

The Control Data people kept 45 percent interest in the venture.

Big business apparently intended to protect its profits at any cost.

Howard Phillips pointed out on February 3, 1986: *"Gulf's corporate executives have also been lobbying on behalf of the Soviet Union urging Congress to reject U.S. aid*

to the UNITA [Angolan anti-communist] freedom fighters."

Suggested Gary Allen sarcastically in May of 1974: *"Having carefully arranged to commit suicide by firing the Communist furnaces while our own are cold, to build Russian tanks and Russian planes and the Russian nuclear industry, and to feed the Russian bear, it is obviously time to provide for the Chinese dragon."*

President Richard M. Nixon and identified Kremlin spy Henry Kissinger paid homage to China's genocide specialist Chairman Mao in 1973.

While wining and dining in Peking, these men began doing business with one of history's worst mass-murderers.

The succinct words of revolutionary Saul Alinsky on July 14, 1986, apply here as elsewhere: *"As for businessmen, I could persuade a capitalist on Friday to bankroll a revolution on*

Saturday that will bring him a profit on Sunday, even though he will be executed on Monday."

There was absolutely no evidence in 1973 to lead anyone to believe Communist Occupied China's revolutionary goals had changed.

Nothing even remotely indicated that the dogmatic Red Chinese were now to be accepted as America's friend and ally.

Yet, the Nixon Administration allowed the criminal Mao regime to obtain Boeing 707 aircraft.

Furthermore, Communist Occupied China's aviation industry was to be developed by Boeing.

Pullman company was given the green light to build ammonia plants worth $130 million -- all on credit!

A Pullman subsidiary contracted to construct eight large plants for the manufacture of synthetic fertilizer.

The U.S. was going to help the arrogant Chinese Reds exploit their massive undersea oil reserves.

Why?

Robert S. Elegant reported in the *Los Angeles Times* of May 20, 1973: *"Because only the United States possesses the deepwater technology and engineering hardware to sink wells in the 400-700 foot depths where most of the oil lies."*

Standard Oil of Ohio was another money-hungry culprit.

It agreed to supply these Marxist-Leninists with their secret process for making orlon, acrylics, and other fibers.

This was willingly done for a blood-thirsty Red regime with an unbelievable track record of terror, torture, devastation, and death.

Communist Occupied China has been allowed to make unlimited purchases of American aerospace, military,  and industrial equipment.

Much of this is paid for with American taxpayer's money from the U.S. Export-Import Bank.

Groveling in the wings and anxious to do business with these Red gangsters are such firms as Textron, McDonnell Douglas, Loral

Corporation, Allied Bendix, RCA, Lockheed and Martin Marietta.

The savage Chinese dictatorship received diplomatic recognition and *Most Favored Nation (MFN)* status in 1979.

None of this was really necessary since American leaders had been quietly doing business with this tyrannical regime for years.

All the Carter Administration did was legalize further unlawful plunder.

Where else other than under Communist sanctioned terrorism has the world witnessed the consistent gang rape and torture of nuns?

The brutalization and mutilation of Christian missionaries?

The burning of churches, with the entire congregation locked inside?

The use of the Red Cross insignia on hospital roofs for bombing and strafing practice?

Private investment in Communist Occupied China exceeded $1 billion in 1986 despite having verifiable knowledge of this.

More than 250 American firms opened business facilities in Peking and elsewhere in Red China.

Minnesota Mining and Manufacturing agreed in 1983 to build a factory in the Red dictatorship.

They were the first American company to take advantage of Communist China's low wages and slave labor.

Their high-tech electrical items and telecommunications equipment parts are manufactured for sale throughout the free world.

No American firm can lose on these apostate, no-risk deals.

Everything is insured by the Overseas Private Investment Corporation.

In other words American taxpayers are forced to pay off any company losses from an investment turned sour in the Red Chinese slave-labor state!

General Electric contracted with Communists Occupied China in August 1985 for five LM-2500 gas turbine engines.

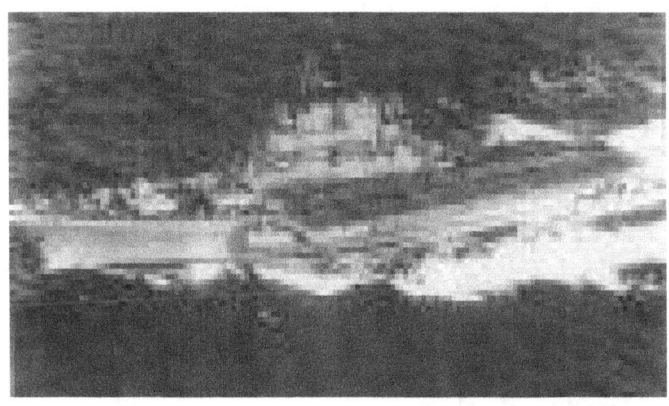

These were to be installed by GE on Red China's Luda-class destroyers.

Red China produced AMC jeeps, courtesy of the American Motors Corporation. Peking just happens to be the District of Columbia's so-called *"Sister City."*

According to *USA Today* on March 17, 1988, Mayor Marion Barry was given the first AMC Jeep Cherokee as it came off the Chinese assembly line, early in 1988.

Greedy businessmen have sold unbelievable amounts of highly strategic merchandise to America's Communist enemies.

Yet no government official or American businessmen had ever been called to task as a traitor.

Not one of these people had ever been prosecuted for treason.

Why?

"It is bad enough when the news media see nothing but progress and light coming out of Red China and endow Deng Xiaoping with godlike qualities of leadership

and wisdom," surmised Senator Barry Goldwater on April 21, 1986, *"but now the [Reagan] Administration seems to accept the same distorted view that Communist China can do no wrong and is a threat to no one."*

Epilogue

The record covering crucial episodes of the McCarthy era has been massively and deliberately distorted from the very beginning!

Conveniently forgotten or deliberately overlooked are the 78 hearings held between 1951 and 1952 by Senator William E. Jenner's (R-Indiana) Senate Internal Security Subcommittee (SISS); the House Committee On Internal Security; the House Un-American Activities Committee (HUAC) under the chairmanship of both Martin Dies (D-Texas) and Francis Walters (D-Pa); the Federal Bureau of Investigation (FBI) under the guidance of J. Edgar Hoover; and other investigating committees and individuals.

Out of all of these investigations one man was selected:

To be stopped!

To be destroyed!

To be made an example!

Why?

So that no one would ever again dare to initiate any investigations into the penetration of our government agencies by communist agents (spies) in the employ of the Soviet Union!

Yes!

An obscure Senator from Wisconsin was deliberately targeted for this purpose!

Joseph McCarthy's incredibly successful investigations panicked those on the political left.

Their reaction was shockingly quick!

Key data was been suppressed, denied and even widely falsified.

This took place in the media, all branches of government and many alleged scholars entrenched in the ivory towers of our institutions of higher learning!

Such misreporting and misrepresentation of the facts continues today.

Much of the misinformation we were (and still are today) so carefully spoon-fed about Senator Joseph McCarthy the man and his investigations was no more than an admixture of uncheckable blovations from deceased third parties and demonstratable falsehoods!

For example, how many innocent people were harmed by McCarthy's revelations?

The correct answer?

Not one!

No!

Not One!

McCarthy's most virulent critics have had more than a half century to produce the names of the hundreds of innocent people they claim were destroyed by the astounding revelations of the Senator from Wisconsin.

Yet those highly skilled propagandists in our media and government and institutions of higher learning have been unable to name even one innocent person they claim was destroyed after being falsely accused by McCarthy!

How many innocent people committed suicide as a result of McCarthy's exposure?

The correct answer?

Not one!

Not one suicide can be attributed to the investigations conducted by McCarthy!

No! Not one!

According to the obscene claims made the highly skilled propagandists in our media, government and scholars entranced in those ivory towers of our colleges and universities there were a rash of suicides with bodies falling constantly of the heads of pedestrians below on the streets of Manhattan!

Once again, McCarthy's most virulent critics have had more than 50 years to produce the names of the hundreds of innocent people they claim committed suicide because of the astounding revelations of the Senator from Wisconsin.

Yet those highly skilled propagandists in our media and government and institutions of higher learning have been unable to name even one innocent person they claim committed suicide after being falsely accused by McCarthy!

No!

Not one!

But there were two suicides on record during the McCarthy period!

Neither was the result of an innocent person who'd been ruined by McCarthy's revelations!

Both were subversives who'd been exposed by McCarthy!

Both were subversives who'd been positively indentified as Kremlin agents!

Lawrence Duggan had been operating in the State Department as a widely known Soviet spy!

He'd been called to testify before a Congressional investigating committee.

Duggan never made it!

He conveniently "fell" from a window high up in a Manhattan skyscraper!

Fell?

Probably not!

He was more than likely pushed from or tossed out of the window by an assassin in the employ of the Soviet Union!

Why?

To make certain he didn't fold under pressure and start naming other Kremlin moles.

Secondly there was the unexpected demise of Harry Dexter White.

This Soviet agent discovered that he was being investigated by J. Edgar Hoover of the FBI!

He died of a sudden heart attack!

Coincidence?

Not hardly!

Was White's death a suicide?

Yes or at least so claimed McCarthy's critics!

Again, not hardly!

Heart attacks can readily be induced with the proper use of certain medicines administered by a hired assassin in the employ of the Kremlin!

Why?

Simply to eliminate anyone who might panic and decide to turncoat and reveal the names of other spies secretly entrenched deeply in the bowels of every branch of our government.

To sum up, most fit into one of three categories:

Conscience lacking incurable liars!

Those with an axe to grind!

Individuals who simply do not know the facts!

If you liked this book in the *None Dare Call It Treason* series then you'll probably also enjoy reading the others!

Gift copies of this book can be ordered at

createspace.com/4215805

Available Titles

None Dare Call It Treason Book 1
The Internal Security Farce!
5.5" x 8.5" 103 pages $4.95
Order from createspace.com/421951

None Dare Call It Treason Book 2
Never Ending Subversion In Government!
5.5" x 8.5" 99 pages $4.95
Order from createspace.com/4216385

None Dare Call It Treason Book 3
America's Subversive State Department
Bloated With Security Risks
5.5" x 8.5" 98 pages $4.95
Order from createspace.com/4216626

None Dare Call It Treason Book 4
America's Illustrious State Department!
It's Machiavellian Misdeeds!
5.5" x 8.5" 106 pages $4.95
Order from createspace.com/4215018

None Dare Call It Treason Book 5
Our Presidents A Major Security Threat!
5.5" x 8.5" 73 pages $4.95
Order from createspace.com/4213501

None Dare Call It Treason Book 6
Presidential Words & Deeds
&Blatant Lies!
5.5" x 8.5" 128 pages $4.95
Order from createspace.com/4213920

None Dare Call It Treason Book 7
Subversives Close To Our Presidents
5.5" x 8.5" 104 pages $4.95
Order from createspace.com/4213931

None Dare Call It Treason Book 8
Henry Kissinger
The Shadowy Untouchable Kremlin Spy!
5.5" x 8.5" 74 pages $4.95

Order from createspace.com/4215805

None Dare Call It Treason Book 9
Inexcusably Arming America's Enemies!
5.5" x 8.5" 102 pages $4.95
Order from createspace.com/4216634

None Dare Call It Treason Book 10
*Inexcusably Financing
America's Enemies!*
5.5" x 8.5" 102 pages $4.95
Order from createspace.com/4216777

None Dare Call It Treason Book 11
*Treasonous   Trade With & Aid To
Enemies Of Freedom!*
5.5" x 8.5" 93 pages $4.95
Order from createspace.com/4216873

None Dare Call It Treason Book 12
*Wholesale Treason During the War
In Vietnam!*
5.5" x 8.5" 120 pages $4.95
Order from createspace.com/4215293

None Dare Call It Treason Book 13
Big Business
& Astounding Acts Of Treason!
5.5" x 8.5" 93 pages $4.95
Order from createspace.com/4215805

None Dare Call It Treason Book 14
Illegally Importing Slave Made Goodies!
5.5" x 8.5" 91 pages $4.95
Order from createspace.com/4215894

None Dare Call It Treason Book 15
The House That Hiss Built
The Anti-American United Nations!
5.5" x 8.5" 117 pages $4.95
Order from createspace.com/4215323

None Dare Call It Treason Book 16
Security Risks in the House and Senate!
5.5" x 8.5" 62 pages $4.95
Order from createspace.com/4213508

None Dare Call It Treason Book 17
The Supreme Court A Devastating
Threat To National Security!

5.5" x 8.5" 90 pages $4.95
Order from createspace.com/4213689

Orders for Resale
40% Off Retail Price

Send Purchase Order to

christianamerica2@yahoo.com

MEET THE AUTHOR

Robert W. Pelton has been writing and lecturing for more than 45 years on political, religious and historical subjects.

He has published more than 100 books including the sensational exposé *Unwanted Dead or Alive – The Greatest Act of Treason in Our History – The betrayal of American POWs Following World War II, Korea and Vietnam.*

Mr, Pelton proudly claims a heritage going all the way back to well before the War for American Independence.

One of Mr. Pelton's ancestors, John Rogers, came to America on the Mayflower and was one of 41 signers of the Mayflower Compact.

Another, John Smith was one of the founders of Jamestown.

Peleg Pelton served as the fifer in the Continental Army at age 18 during the Battle of Saratoga (1777) and again in Yorktown (1781).

Captain Peter Hager was Commander of the Old Stone Fort in Schoharie, New York, in 1780.

Another, Captain Bezaleel Tyler fought in the only Revolutionary War Battle taking place in Sullivan County, New York.

Mr. Pelton is a member of Sons of the Revolution (SOR), and Sons of the American Revolution (SAR).